SUNDAY MORNING LIVE

VOLUME 2

Willow Creek Resources is a publishing partnership between Zondervan Publishing House and the Willow Creek Association. Willow Creek Resources includes drama sketches, small group curricula, training material, videos, and many other specialized ministry resources.

Willow Creek Association is an international network of churches ministering to the unchurched. Founded in 1992, the Willow Creek Association serves churches through conferences, seminars, regional roundtables, consulting, and ministry resource materials. The mission of the Association is to assist churches in reestablishing the priority and practice of reaching lost people for Christ through church ministries targeted to seekers.

For conference and seminar information please write to:

Willow Creek Association
P.O. Box 3188
Barrington, Illinois 60011-3188

SUNDAY MORNING LIVE

VOLUME 2

A Collection of Drama Sketches
from Willow Creek Community Church

Edited by Steve Pederson

ZondervanPublishingHouse
Grand Rapids, Michigan
A Division of HarperCollinsPublishers

WILLOW CREEK
RESOURCES

Sunday Morning Live: Volume 2
Copyright © 1992 by Willow Creek Community Church
All rights reserved

Requests for information should be addressed to:
Zondervan Publishing House
Grand Rapids, Michigan 49530

Library of Congress Cataloging-in-Publication Data

Sunday morning live.

   1. Christian drama, American. I. Pederson, Steve.
II. Willow Creek Community Church (South Barrington, Ill.)
PS627.R4S8   1992   812'.54080382   92-26029
ISBN 0-310-59221-6 (v. 1)
ISBN 0-310-61361-2 (v. 2)

Edited by Lori J. Walburg
Cover design by Cheryl Van Andel

Printed in the United States of America

92 93 94 95 96 / ❖ CH / 10 9 8 7 6 5 4 3 2 1

To the people of
Willow Creek Community Church

We could not ask for a more supportive
and encouraging audience

Contents

About the Contributors

Donna Hinkle Lagerquist has been a part of the Willow Creek drama team for eleven years and a writer for five. Her sketch *Stolen Jesus* is being adapted into a Canadian Television Christmas special. She and her husband, Paul, are expecting their first child. They live in Cary, Illinois.

Judson Poling was drama director at Willow Creek for five years. He continues to serve on Willow Creek's staff in the area of small group leadership training. Judson is also co-author of the *Walking With God Series,* Willow Creek's small group curriculum. Judson holds a Master of Divinity degree from Trinity Evangelical Divinity School. He lives with his wife, Debra, and their two children in Algonquin, Illinois.

Sharon Sherbondy has been a member of the drama team for fourteen years and a writer for eight. Her drama ministry has taken her throughout the United States and abroad. She is a co-author of *Super Sketches for Youth Groups,* a finalist for the Gold Medallion Book Award. She home schools her two children and lives with her husband, Steve, in Elgin, Illinois.

Introduction

In 1975, Willow Creek Community Church began in a rented movie theater in suburban Chicago. Founded with the expressed purpose of reaching the nonchurched, today Willow Creek attracts upwards of 15,000 people to its weekend "seeker services."

Since the beginning, drama has been an integral part of Willow Creek's outreach. Different from traditional church drama, these sketches are short, six- to eight-minute, contemporary vignettes, rooted in real-life experience. Today many churches all over the country, both large and small, are using these sketches as a powerful part of their ministry.

The Message "Set Up"

These sketches are not intended to stand on their own. Rather, they are used to create interest in an issue by grabbing the attention of the audience and getting them to identify with the characters. Also, the sketches do not provide easy answers but instead raise questions, which the pastor then seeks to answer in the message. Much of the material in this volume may seem "secular," in that there is no specific "Christian" content in the sketch itself. However, when performed in connection with a biblically based message that addresses the same question or problem, the sketch takes on spiritual significance.

This separation of drama and message is a major difference between Willow Creek's approach to drama and that traditionally taken by many churches. While difficult for some people to accept, such a separation is supported by dramatic tradition throughout history. Dorothy Sayers, Christian playwright and novelist, summed it up well: "Playwrights are not evangelists." A dictum frequently repeated to aspiring playwrights is "if you have a message, send it to Western Union." At Willow Creek we try not to abuse drama as an art form by manipulating it to preach a message. Simply put, the sketches clarify the "bad news" so the pastor can bring the "good news."

The Audience "Set Up"

A sketch cannot "set up" a message if viewers do not, in some way, see themselves mirrored in the action. Drama works because people experience vicariously what characters act out on stage. We want to engage not only the minds, but also the emotions of our audience. And drama, which results in high identification, appeals to people's hearts as well as their heads.

At Willow Creek we use contemporary "slice of life" drama, rather than enacted biblical stories, because people more readily identify with characters who act and talk like they do and who confront the same daily issues. This approach helps us earn the right to be heard, because our seekers realize that the church is in touch with the real world, where real people live, work, and struggle.

A sketch that we have performed often in many different settings is *For Better or Worse*. The audience response is always the same. Spouses laughingly elbow each other as Steve, who has one thing on his mind, tries to "romance" his wife. However, when Paula breaks down, expressing hurt and frustration at being the "last thought of the day," the elbowing usually stops. The identification is so strong, the tension so true to life, that a light-hearted poke at a spouse becomes inappropriate. Such a sketch, with its honest look at marriage, primes an audience to want to hear a pastor present what tools the Bible provides to help navigate relational breakdowns.

We've discovered that the degree of audience identification directly parallels what we call the "reality factor." Drama earns credibility with an audience when it is honest and truthful in how it handles material. If drama comes off simplistic and naïve, or presents clichéd, easy answers, it will not produce the desired result.

Great Expectations is a sketch we developed for the message topic, "The Mystery of Unanswered Prayer." Our goal was to deal honestly with what happens when Christians, because of some negative life experience, begin to believe that God is immune to their pain.

The couple in *Great Expectations* joyfully anticipate the arrival of their adopted son. But at the last moment the adoptive mother changes her mind. After dealing for years with the pain of infertility, this news is almost more than the couple can bear. As the sketch progresses, the woman grows increasingly angry. She cannot understand how God could "dangle a carrot . . . only to yank it away." Her anger and confusion is so deep that at the emotional climax of the scene she lashes out, "I hate that girl . . . I hate God!" While such a sentiment may seem at cross purposes with what the church is trying to accomplish, anyone who has

experienced a similar level of pain will readily identify with such confusion and anger. At the end of the sketch, the woman asks, "Where have our prayers been going?" and confesses that she hasn't got "any faith left." Rather than preach, her husband painfully and somewhat defeatedly says, "We'll just keep praying . . . we'll just keep trying."

If we try to give easy answers when we dramatize such life experiences, we will diminish the emotional impact and power of what we produce. It is far better to simply be honest with the pain, and let the pastor provide the biblical perspective.

If drama for seekers is to be effective in the church, we must be passionately committed to being real, warts and all. We must avoid easy answers, because they ultimately don't help, even if they sound good. Seekers and believers alike want truth, not a sugarcoated, sanitized version of reality.

In his book *Open Windows*, in a chapter entitled "Pitfalls of Christian Writing," Philip Yancey laments:

> Sometimes when I read
> Christian books, especially in

the fields of fiction and biography, I have a suspicion that characters have been strangely lobotomized. . . . Just as a lobotomy flattens out emotional peaks and valleys, Christian writers can tend to safely reduce life's tensions and strains to a more acceptable level. . . . A perverse fear of overstatement keeps us confined to that flatland realm of "safe" emotions and tensions—a fear that seems incredible in light of the biblical model.

The cause of Christ would be well served if the church would listen to Yancey. For it is truth-telling (which isn't very safe) that not only gives ministry integrity, but also opens up seekers to the possibility of transformation through the power of the Gospel.

Getting Started

The sketch format is a fairly easy way for any church, regardless of size, to begin using drama. A little time, a few simple props, a couple of actors (in some cases just one), and a director are all the necessary elements.

Because sketches are short, the time demand for rehearsals is not excessive. Typically, we spend about four to five hours rehearsing each one. If you are working with relatively inexperienced people, however, it would probably be wise to plan more time. Our four hours is divided into two rehearsals. The actors pick up their scripts one week before the performance. Our first rehearsal is early in the week, during which time we discuss the characters and work out the basic movement (blocking). Because we have only two rehearsals, we ask the actors to memorize the script prior to this rehearsal, with the goal of being off the script by the end of the two-hour session.

For the second rehearsal—in our case, before it is performed for the first service—we rehearse one and a half hours, working on stage with the hand props and furniture we'll be using. During this time we polish the movement, work on character consistency, pacing, and the rise and fall of the action. If movement doesn't look natural because an actor is having a hard time making it look motivated, we change it. After we're off the stage, we run lines or work problem areas of blocking for an additional half to full hour. We also try to relax and enjoy each other's company before the service begins.

For props, we use only that which is absolutely necessary. In other words, we don't use furniture to establish setting, but only if it fulfills a necessary function in the sketch. If, for example, a phone is needed, we would use an end table to set it on. But if nothing needs to sit on the end table, why use one? Typically we do not use door or window units. If a window is called for, we mime it. However, rather than mime the opening and closing of an imaginary door, which gets cumbersome, the actors simply enter a room, a convention which an audience seems to accept.

A simple rule of thumb, then, for props and scenic pieces is to keep them simple and rely on the audience's imagination to fill in the details. Not only is this an easier route, but—unless you have a professional set designer—it is also the most effective. Furthermore, since props usually need to be set in

place before a sketch and removed afterwards, the simpler you can keep it, the better.

While the technical elements necessary to produce a good sketch are fairly basic, assembling the right actors and someone to "lead the charge" might prove more challenging. Talent in drama, unlike the other arts, is somewhat difficult to assess quickly. If someone cannot sing a song or play an instrument, it is readily evident, but acting talent is more difficult to define. To further complicate the matter, drama seems to attract people who have an affinity for the arts but who lack specific talent or training. Someone reasons, "I can't sing, or play the piano, but I think I can act." Indeed, maybe this person has acting ability, but too often such people are drawn to drama because it appears relatively "easy," at least compared to the other arts. But doing drama well is more difficult than it appears. Unfortunately, many well-intentioned people, because they know little about the craft of drama, have not helped further the cause of drama in the church. God is not served when drama is done poorly.

Therefore, before getting serious about drama, even short sketches, the church must find a competent drama director. This person needs to have adequate people skills, the ability to assess acting talent, and an understanding of the basics of stage direction. If someone possesses great drama instincts but lacks formal training, it would be a wise investment for a church to enroll this person in some courses in acting and directing at a local college. A good course in directing can provide many of the basic principles necessary for staging drama effectively.

Having formally trained actors is an advantage, but most churches do not have this luxury—all the more reason to have someone with skill and training leading the team. Over time, talented lay people with good dramatic instincts can develop into strong performers, even if they have no previous drama experience, but their growth will be severely limited if their directors do not have sufficient training.

And finally, a word of encouragement. Once a person has understood some basic principles of theatre—as simple as this sounds—that person learns to do drama by *doing* drama. Even the most inexperienced actors and directors can improve, as long as they are willing to learn from their mistakes.

Throughout our many years of doing drama at Willow Creek, we have made numerous mistakes. We still do. In the earlier years, for example, too many of our scripts were "preachy," and therefore stilted and manipulated. Today, periodically, we do a script that we think will work, but it ends up falling flat, due to a lack of conflict, identification, humor, or any number of factors. Sometimes it is particularly frustrating because it's difficult to figure out exactly why a script appeared not to "go over." Such is the business of doing original drama. But as long as we try to learn from each experience, over time we improve the quality and increase our understanding of the craft of drama.

It is our hope that the "tested" resources in *Sunday Morning Live Volume 2,* and others in volumes to follow, will provide you with at least one of the necessary elements for doing drama—the script.

Based on our experience at Wil-low Creek, these sketches have worked well. We pray they will work well for you, too.

Steve Pederson
Drama Director
Willow Creek
   Community Church

The
Offering

It's time for the offering, and four people express their reasons for giving or not giving. The first chooses not to give because she doubts how wisely the church uses what it gets. The second gives because of the recognition he might receive. The third, driven by guilt, hates giving because she feels God is never satisfied with what she offers. The fourth enjoys giving because it is his opportunity to say thanks to God.

SUGGESTED TOPICS: giving, tithing

CHARACTERS:

Woman #1	a skeptical giver
Man #1	an ostentatious giver
Woman #2	a guilt-ridden giver
Man #2	a joyful giver

PROPS: pew or chairs, offering plate, checkbook, pen, wallet, purse, credit cards, earrings, rings

The Offering

Judson Poling

Setting: *Four people in a row, sitting on a pew or in individual chairs. Each person "comes to life" as the plate is passed to him or her.*

Woman #1: Well, it's that time in the service again — the offering. You're barely settled and they're passing the plate. What do they need such a big one for? Is this some kind of a hint to put a lot in or what? I suppose I ought to contribute something. The church has to pay its bills too. And these are comfortable seats, I will have to admit that. *(beginning to be suspicious)* Come to think of it, there's a lot of nice things they've got here: *(You should adjust these next few lines to describe your church. The following is what we used.)* Get a load of all this glass — as much as in the United Terminal — closed-circuit television, and what's with this atrium-lobby thing? Looks like the Embassy Suites. This stuff ain't cheap. *(growing suspicion)* I bet when you become a member they really put the pressure on you to give all the time. This place must be rolling in the dough! What good is my little measly couple of bucks going to do? Besides, how do I know where my money's going anyways? You can't be too careful these days. There might be some scam here. Now if *I* use my money, at least I'll know what it's going for. I'm sure you understand, God, if I take a pass this morning. From the looks of this place compared to my living room, I need this money a whole lot more than they do. *(Passes offering plate to the next person, then freezes.)*

Man #1: *(pompous and affected)* Ah, yes. The offering. What a wonderful time of the service. There's something about being able to *participate* in what's going on here. To be part of funding this great work of God. *(Starts to write a check with pride.)* A *very, very large* part. I amaze myself with my generosity. And I just know I could be such an example to others. *(thinks)* Of course, how can I be an example if they don't know what I'm doing? I certainly wouldn't want to *tell* anyone what I give—that would be too obvious. *(gets an idea)* 'Course, if I don't fold my check—I could lay it face up on the top for everybody in the row to see. Maybe I should put it on the rim—then they could see it better. Oh, but it might fall off. *(thinks)* Hey, but that would be perfect! Then the people in the row in front who pick it up could see it too. And they'd have to pass it around to have it catch up to the plate and then many more people would see it . . . and be inspired! *(really on a roll now)* And then if they didn't get it to the plate in time the person on the end would have to stand up *(does so)* and call out to the usher, *(waving check)* "Oh sir, sir! There's a very large check from *(looks at check, reads it off)* a Mr. William Tyler, 7432 Winfield Lane, that I'm sure the church couldn't do without this week." *(very excited)* And then the pastor would see what's going on and ask me to come up front and then make me honorary chairman of the Deacons right there . . . *(off in fantasyland, comes back, sits)* What a joy to be a tool in God's hand. *(passes the plate, freezes)*

Woman #2: *(very neurotic)* Oh no—the offering plate. I just hate this part of the service. *(Looks in plate and says)* "Feed me!" *(as in the film,* Little Shop of Horrors. *Resumes her own voice).* I bet everybody's watching me. *(paranoid)* I bet the couple behind is looking over my shoulder to see how much I'm putting in. *(After fearful pause, turns around quickly.)* Stop staring at me! *(turns front sheepishly)* There's nobody there—I'm in the last row! Why am I so paranoid? What's the big deal about giving to the Lord? I know I should give more. *(to God)* I'm trying Lord—what do you expect of me? *(to self)* Listen to me. I'm riddled with guilt. Just because I didn't give anything that week I was on vacation two years ago. *(new thought, to God)*

Okay God, I give up. You caught me red-handed. Yesterday I didn't separate my trash; I didn't recycle! *(taking wallet out of her purse)* Here, just take my whole wallet. *(places it in plate)* Take my credit cards. *(dropping loose cards in the plate)* Go ahead—there's still a few hundred bucks on 'em. *(brief pause, to self)* It's not good enough! I have to let it all out! *(to God)* Here, take my earrings—this is for lying to my mother when I was thirteen. *(Throws earrings into offering plate.)* And here's my rings—these ought to cover the night of senior prom. *(also tosses into plate)* And here's my shoes. *(into plate)* Yes, I went ten miles over the speed limit on my way over here. I'll walk home barefoot on the gravel just to prove how sorry I am! There God—is that enough? *(Panting. Eventually gains some composure, low voice, slowly.)* I hate this part of the service. *(passes the plate, freezes)*

Man #2: *(sees shoes, picks one up, looks at woman, puzzled, then sets shoes back in the plate)* Well, here it is. A chance to say thanks. You know, Lord, this has been a good week. Every day I've had enough food, every night I've gone to bed in a warm house, every morning I've had a hot shower . . . well, except for Thursday, when the kids got up early. But all in all, I've had a lot of good things come my way this week. And I'm glad I have a chance to show you that while I know I matter to you, you matter to me too. To think two years ago I would've been in the office on Sunday morning, just building my little business. What a prison! But here I am today. And now, in a tangible way, I get to show you something of how much I appreciate your presence in my life. This is for *you,* Lord . . . *(Reaches for wallet, not there. Checks other pockets, not there. Nervous laugh, embarrassed.)* i left my wallet in the car.

All: *(in unison, turning their heads to look at him)* Sure, you did!

Blackout

A
Nice Guy

Glen has recently landed a job teaching at the school his friend Bill attended as a child. When Glen takes Bill to see his classroom, Bill remembers how he and his friends bullied another kid from the class. The confession that ensues helps Bill deal with the guilt he's been carrying for years.

SUGGESTED TOPICS: sin, confession, the haunting past

CHARACTERS:

Glen	an enthusiastic grade school teacher
Bill	the nice guy who doesn't feel very nice

PROPS: two student desks, teacher's desk and chair, two boxes of teachers' supplies, flag (radiator and blackboard can be imagined)

A
Nice Guy

Donna Hinkle Lagerquist

Setting: *A grade school room, established by two students' desks and a teacher's desk, perhaps a flag. Glen and Bill enter carrying boxes of supplies.*

Glen: You can just set that on one of the desks . . . thanks.

Bill: *(looking around)* Boy, the saying "it's a small world," is all too true here.

Glen: It's hard to believe that people this small can even function outside their homes . . . let alone learn something!

Bill: It's hard to imagine I was ever this small . . . that I was sitting looking out these same windows seventeen years ago! I can't believe you landed a job here!

Glen: Bill, have faith . . . I'm a great teacher!

Bill: No . . . I mean here . . . at my grade school!

Glen: I don't think my alma mater would ever hire me . . . I was a terror in grade school.

Bill: It even smells the same.

Glen: Really?

Bill: Yeah, a combination of milk, paste, and mimeographed papers . . . Remember those?

Both: Dittos!

Bill: We used to get high on them.

Glen: *(laughs, turns, mimes erasing a blackboard)* Goodbye, Mrs. Schuetz! And thank you for taking maternity leave in the middle of the school year . . . when I needed a job!

Bill: *(still looking around, pondering)* I remember one girl . . . Mary Ann Blodgett . . . sat in the back there . . . She always smelled like formaldehyde or something.

Glen: Don't tell me, her dad was a mortician.

Bill: Her mom worked at a dry cleaners, and she'd go with her until school started. But we made up some great stories about her dad being a mad scientist in her basement like Frankenstein or something . . . *(smiles, then gets serious)*

Glen: *(Turns his back to write his name on board. As he does this, Bill notices the radiator — can be mimed—downstage and goes over to look at it.)* "Welcome Mr. Novak." It's pretty sad to have to make your own welcome banner . . . huh? Bill? *(Notices him kneeling down focusing on the radiator.)* What are you doing?

Bill: It's still here! I can't believe it was never replaced!

Glen: What? You scratched your name in the radiator? *(sarcastic)* You delinquent you!

Bill: No . . . Bobby Heaver pulled it loose . . . seventeen years ago. . . . It's still pulled up some from the floor . . . *(sits back, reflective)* I figured someone would have fixed it by now.

Glen: *(half joking, half wondering)* Bill . . . it's okay . . . I'm sure if it presented a danger to the kids it would have been fixed. Bobby's off the hook! Wanna help me hang these posters?

Bill: He hung himself.

Glen: Excuse me?

Bill: Bobby hung himself . . . I guess he is off the hook.

Glen: (confused) You mean a fifth grader hung himself in your class . . . from a radiator? I don't get it . . .

Bill: No . . . two years ago . . . he hung himself two years ago. My mom read about it in the paper and called me. He did it at home, I guess . . . (getting upset) Man, Glen, if kids in your class are mean to one another, if they're picking on someone, do you stop them? I mean do you care enough to stop them? Or do you just sit there and let it happen? Do you do anything? Tell me you do something!

Glen: (taken aback by Bill's intensity) It depends on what's going on . . . but yeah, I stop it, and usually help the kids work it out . . .

Bill: (accusingly) Usually?

Glen: Whoa, Bill . . . what's going on?

Bill: Seventeen years ago me and some of my buddies tied Bobby Heaver to that radiator.

Glen: Kids do stuff like that to kids all the time . . .

Bill: We weren't playing cowboys and Indians or cops and robbers, Glen. We tied Bobby up because he was little and skinny and talked funny. We decided that wasn't cool, and we let him know it. I let him know that every day at school, Glen. I reminded him that he was weird. I don't know why I did it . . . I guess it made me feel real tough . . . real "big." Now it makes me sick.

Glen: Hey, Bill . . .

Bill: Back then we used the word homo. I didn't even know what it meant . . . except that he was different. "Homo Heaver" is what I called him . . . what we chanted as he walked by us in a line we formed in front of the school door. It was horrible. I can only imagine how he dreaded coming to school . . .

Glen: *(realizing he needs to talk)* What happened the day you tied him to the radiator?

Bill: *(with difficulty)* We decided we needed to find out for ourselves if he was really a boy. I brought some rope from the garage. I grabbed his feet, and Doug and Andy each took an arm and gagged him and we carried him in and tied him to the radiator before class started one day. *(painfully)* We dropped his pants and left him tied there for the whole class to see . . . and laugh at. When the bell rang, we all ran inside. Bobby had struggled so hard to get loose that his ankles were bleeding and the bottom of the radiator was pulled up a bit from the floor . . . but he didn't cry. I remember looking at him, mad at him and almost afraid of him, because he wasn't crying . . . he wouldn't do it . . . he wouldn't give in.

Glen: What happened?

Bill: The teacher sent him down to the nurse and sent us down to the principal. I got a few detentions. My mom grounded me . . . but it wasn't punishment enough. *(pause)* I ruined his life. He was never the same after that. When I heard he killed himself I figured he couldn't bear not fitting in any longer. *(pause)* You know . . . people think I'm such a nice guy . . . but I'm not! I feel like I killed him, Glen. I really feel like I murdered someone!

Glen: *(emphatically)* You've been carrying this around for a long time, Bill.

Bill: Seventeen years. *(pause)* Hey, I'm sorry, Glen. I mean, here I am ruining the best thing that's happened to you this year. I . . .

Glen: It's okay . . . really . . . I'm glad I was here . . . and I'm glad you told me . . . *(realizing Bill needs to be alone)* I gotta go pick up a few things down at the office . . . you wanna come with or . . .

Bill: No . . . ah, unless you need me . . . I'll wait here . . .

Glen: I'll be back. *(leaves)*

(Bill sits on the desk for a moment, then looks to make sure Glen has gone. He gets up, slowly crosses over to the radiator and sits down on the floor in front of it. He reaches out his hand, touching it.)

Bill: *(slowly, moved)* I'm sorry, Heaver . . . I'm sorry.

Lights slowly fade

For Better
or Worse

It's 11:00 p.m., and Steve's asleep on the couch. Paula heads for bed when suddenly Steve wakes up and wants to "you know what." What ensues is a humorous but also honest look at the frustration Paula experiences from being "the last thought of the day."

SUGGESTED TOPICS: marriage, romance

CHARACTERS:

| Paula | a wife who wants to feel cherished |
| Steve | a husband who lacks sensitivity |

PROPS: couch, cushions, remote control, newspaper, wristwatch

For Better or Worse

Sharon Sherbondy

Setting: *Steve is lying on the couch sleeping. A newspaper is on top of him. T.V. is on, with hockey game playing. Cushions on floor. Evening lighting.*

Paula: *(Enters. Sees cushions on floor. Shows frustration. Looks at T.V., then at Steve, then picks up remote and turns off T.V. Looks at Steve, then at watch. She drops remote on Steve's chest and turns to leave. This awakens him.)*

Steve: *(yawning)* Where you going?

Paula: To bed.

Steve: What time is it?

Paula: 11:15. Good night. *(gives him a quick kiss)*

Steve: *(grabs her hand)* Hey, it's been a while.

Paula: *(knows what he means, but pretends otherwise)* Yeah, well, after about seventeen hours I'm usually due for another night's sleep.

Steve: *(pulls her back)* I'm talking about . . . you know.

(Paula grabs side of couch and gasps.)

Steve: *(alarmed)* Honey, what's wrong?

Paula: I can't catch my breath.

Steve: *(jumps up)* Paula!

Paula: I'll be okay. *(struggling to catch her breath)* This always happens when I'm *(drops act, sarcastic)* swept off my feet.

Steve: Very funny.

Paula: I'm going to bed.

Steve: I'll be right up.

Paula: I'll be asleep.

Steve: I'll wake you up.

Paula: I'll lock the door.

Steve: I'll break it down.

Paula: *(stops and turns)* Now, *that* I'd stay awake for.

Steve: Hey, what's your problem?

Paula: My problem?

Steve: Yeah, I want to make love to my wife and . . .

Paula: Oh, is that what you want to do? Make love to your wife? And I thought you were just looking for something to do during half-time.

Steve: Hockey doesn't have half-time.

Paula: *(picks up cushion and throws it at him)* Ugh.

Steve: Will you stop it? I'm getting real tired of your attitude.

Paula: And I'm getting real tired of being the last thought of the day or a cure for your insomnia.

Steve: *(frustrated)* You are not a cure for my insomnia!

Paula: But I *am* the last thought of the day.

Steve: Will you give me a break!

Paula: Well, it sure feels that way. You come home, eat dinner, and then park yourself on that couch for the rest of the night, snoring between the headlines and hockey pucks. You don't say a . . . a meaningful word to me all night . . .

Steve: *(conceding, sort of)* All right. What do you want me to do?

Paula: Steve, you know very well . . .

Steve: Okay. *(somewhat sarcastic)* You want to talk, we'll talk.

Paula: I don't want to talk . . .

Steve: You just said . . .

Paula: Doggone it, Steve, I want you to . . . *(hard to have to say)* notice me, to make me feel . . . special, important.

Steve: Oh, you want me to "woo" you. I thought I got all that stuff out of the way when we were dating. *(Paula picks up cushion.)* I didn't mean that. Paula, come on.

Paula: No. You want me, you know how to get me.

Steve: *(frustrated, pause)* Well, I can't do it if you're going to stare at me.

Paula: What, do you want me to go into the other room?

Steve: Well . . .

Paula: Forget it. *(starts to leave)*

Steve: *(cutting her off)* Okay. Okay. Just— just give me a minute. It's been a long time since I've done any "wooing." *(pause)* Well, let's at least sit down and get comfy. *(She complies, but reluctantly. There's a pause, then she turns, looks at him, big smile, as though to say, "Okay, let's see how he does.")* You, uh, look . . . nice . . . tonight. *(pained)* Your shirt's . . . pretty.

(pause) Your pants, uh, fit. *(She cannot believe what he just said.)* You're wearing . . . Your makeup looks nice. Your hair smells good. Your skin feels soft. How am I doing?

Paula: Great . . . if I were a well-dressed cocker spaniel!

Steve: What did I do?

Paula: Steve, how many times do we have to have this conversation? You're not mentally deficient. At least, you weren't until we got married.

Steve: Paula, I gave it my best "woo," okay?

Paula: *(seriously)* This is not funny, Steve. *(turns away hurt)*

Steve: Okay. I'm sorry.

Paula: *(pause, upset)* I can't just turn it on. And I don't want to. I want you to be interested in me, take time out for me. I don't want to be your last thought of the day.

Steve: I already told you . . .

Paula: What do you call this? It's 11:15 at night. And I feel angry when I say yes and I feel guilty when I say no. *(pause)* But most of all, I feel hurt. *(Begins to break down; he goes to hug her.)* And don't hug me. You don't know how to hug or cuddle without . . . wanting more.

Steve: *(long pause, then very sincerely)* Honey, I'm sorry. *(pause, then tentative)* How was work today?

Paula: *(distant)* It was okay.

Steve: *(pause)* Did you get that document finished? What was it you were working on?

Paula: *(still a bit distant)* A proposal for Jim Barnes.

Steve: How'd it go?

Paula: He accepted it.

Steve: Great.

Paula: Yeah. *(beginning to warm up)* I was pretty happy.

Steve: And it looks like you talked to Jenny.

Paula: Yeah. I finally talked her into wearing just *one* pound of blue eye shadow.

Steve: *(points to paper)* Speaking of proposals, did you—

Paula: *(cutting him off)* Thanks.

Steve: Thanks? For what?

Paula: For understanding . . . for trying.

Steve: Okay, I'm a slow learner. After all, it's only been twelve years. Paula . . . *(She looks at him.)* I love you.

Paula: *(with tears)* I love you, too. *(They embrace.)*

Lights fade out

No More Womb

This sketch examines the issues facing children today. The scene opens on a set of fraternal twins who are still inside the womb. After some prenatal sibling rivalry, the twins grow increasingly concerned about what they'll confront in the world outside. When they learn of the threats they will face, such as AIDS and abuse, they end up preferring the womb over the world.

SUGGESTED TOPICS: the world children face, fear of the unknown

CHARACTERS:
> **Boy**
> **Girl**

PROPS: a womb: or muslin "bean bag," stuffed with packing styrofoam "peanuts," approximately ten feet in diameter. Two twelve-feet-long umbilical cords, approximately one inch in diameter (tied around actors' waists and attached to womb). Recording of heartbeat sound.

COSTUMES: baby blue sweats for the boy, pink for the girl.

No More Womb

Donna Hinkle Lagerquist

Setting: *Twins—one boy, one girl in womb sleeping. Boy wakes restless and ready to be born. Sound of a heart beating under. (Note: avoid having adult actors mimic kids or babies. It works much better for them to be "adults" in their actions and costumes.)*

Boy: *(in style of Robin Williams in the film* Good Morning, Vietnam*)* Good morning, Mom! *(up on his knees)* Hey, c'mon out there—get a move on. Today is the big day! *(Heartbeat fades.)*

Girl: *(waking)* Hey—quit hogging all the amniotic fluid! *(Rolls over, trying to go back to sleep.)*

Boy: Aren't you tired of just lying around here maturing? C'mon! *(Starts singing "Happy Birthday" as he pokes at and tickles his sister.)*

Girl: Please settle down! Can't you feel Mommy is resting?

Boy: Not for long! *(stands, yells)* Let me out of here! *(Heart beats faster.)*

Girl: *(getting up)* Come on, settle down. You're gonna— *(both fall backward together)* Never mind, she's up. *(Listens against "wall." Heartbeat fades.)* Oh, now she's having Dad feel for you . . . kick for him!

Boy: (crosses arms) No . . . I don't wanna.

Girl: (rolls eyes) Oh, you are so immature. Well, I'll kick for him. (She throws her arm out as though punching the wall.)

Boy: Hey, watch the cord!

Girl: I want Daddy to feel close to us. We'll need all the help we can get when we're born.

Boy: And today's the day! (Sings again, trying to irritate his sister: "happy birthday to you, happy birthday to me," etc.)

Girl: (angry) Quiet—we are not being born today.

Boy: Yes, we are. (louder) Happy birthday to you . . .

Girl: (grabs his arm) Remember that thumb you discovered? Why don't you use it? Man, sometimes I wish your lungs had never developed.

Boy: That's not nice. I'm telling Mom. (stands) Mommy!

Girl: (stands) Would you be quiet!

(Loud rumbling sound—they both fall backwards and start rolling around as they say the following:)

Girl: (scared) What's happening?

Boy: (scared) I don't know . . .

Girl: Maybe it's a new kind of Kegel exercise.

Boy: I don't think so.

Girl: I'm scared.

Boy: Do you think we're being born?

Girl: I don't know—I've never done it before . . .

Boy: Well, if we are, then (pushing her forward) you go first.

Girl: (pushing him forward) No, you go first . . .

Boy: No, you . . .

Girl: No, you go.

Boy: Let's go together.

(They dive forward, assuming a position like Superman in flight. Rumbling sound stops.)

Girl: *(pause)* Do you smell that? *(sniffs)*

(Boy sniffs cord.)

Girl & Boy: Chicken Fajitas and Salsa!

Girl: We're not in labor—we're *indigestion!*

(Laughing and dancing around, then both plop down, sitting once again.)

Girl: Hey, for someone who *wanted* to be born, you sure acted like a baby.

Boy: I was just surprised . . . that's all. *(Girl starts to get upset.)* What's wrong— too many spices coming through your cord?

Girl: No, that's not it.

Boy: Well, what is it then?

Girl: I . . . I don't want to go.

Boy: Where?

Girl: Out . . . out there.

Boy: Remember hearing Mom say this is a time of limitless opportunities for kids?

Girl: What's so good about that?

Boy: *(trying to come up with evidence)* We can be whatever we want, do whatever we want, go wherever we want . . . we don't have to worry about the cold war—and now we can even manage our cholesterol.

Girl: Oh, big deal. "Limitless opportunities" means limitless decisions and pressures. *(increasingly upset)* What if we don't pass the entrance exam to one of those prestigious nursery schools? How will we ever get into Harvard?

Boy: Okay, okay. Take it easy, or you will send Mom into labor.

Girl: What if our peers think we're geeks because we can't afford Reebok Pumps or Guess jeans?

Boy: Mom and Dad don't want us to be "social rejects." If they can't buy it, they'll hit up the grandparents for it.

Girl: What if our grandparents are dead . . . or dysfunctional? Or what if our parents are dysfunctional because their parents were dysfunctional, and what if they want to ship us off to some boarding school because they don't have time for us. What if—

Boy: *(cutting her off)* What if, what if . . . will you stop with all the "What if's"? *(He's physically agitated.)*

Girl: Watch the cord, will you? And move over. I don't have enough room.

Boy: Womb.

Girl: That's what I said.

Boy: Well, you've got more womb than I do.

Girl: Do not! *(hits him)*

Boy: Do too! *(hits her)*

Girl: Do not! *(hits him)*

Boy: Do too! *(hits her)*

Girl: See, see, we're competing already. And when we're out it'll only get worse.

Boy: What do you mean?

Girl: With honor rolls and athletic ribbons, our physical appearance . . . what if one of us is ugly *(he feels for his nose)* or uncoordinated? *(He tries to pat his head and rub his stomach*

at the same time.) What if you do a cartwheel before I do?

Boy: *(beginning to get the idea)* What if you kick a soccer ball better than me?

Girl: What if we can't handle sibling rivalry?

Boy: It's peer rivalry I wonder about.

Girl: What about disease, what about . . . *(stops)*

Boy: What? What about what?

Girl: Cancer, what if we get cancer from, from a waste dump . . .

Boy: From a hole in the ozone . . .

Girl: From secondary cigarette smoke. Or worse yet, what about . . . *(Both look at each other.)*

Girl & Boy: AIDS.

Boy: *(beginning to cuddle fearfully together, dissonant chords are played under)* Or we could get stolen by a stranger . . .

Girl: Used in pornography . . .

Boy: Battered by our own parents . . .

Girl: Let's not go.

Boy: Yeah, let's not go. *(Pause, hears an ominous rumbling, looks up.)* But wait . . .

Girl: What?

Boy: I don't think we have a choice.

Lights slowly fade out

Great Expectations

It seems as if Kathy and Greg's endless prayers have finally been answered. In a few hours they will be parents. Then, unexpectedly, the birth mother changes her mind about the adoption. Kathy and Greg are again left childless and wondering why God hasn't answered their prayers.

SUGGESTED TOPICS: unanswered prayer, disappointment, storms of life

CHARACTERS:

Kathy	anxious to be a mom
Deb	a friend who shares Kathy's joy
Greg	Kathy's husband

PROPS: couch, wrapped gift for baby, baby outfit

Great Expectations

Sharon Sherbondy

Setting: *Two women, Kathy and Deb, sitting on a living room couch. Kathy is opening a gift.*

Kathy: Oh Deb, our first gift. This is so nice of you.

Deb: Hey, it's the least I can do.

Kathy: *(holding up a Chicago Bears outfit for a baby)* Oh, look at this. It's adorable.

Deb: I fell in love with it the moment I saw it.

Kathy: Can you believe that anything is this small? I just hope I know what to do with it once I get it.

Deb: It?

Kathy: I mean him. Him! Oh, Deb, I can hardly believe it's happening.

Deb: You've waited a long time for this.

Kathy: It seems like a lifetime. Now, after all we've been through, our prayers are finally answered.

Deb: If it had been me I would have given up a long time ago.

Kathy: Listen, there were plenty of low moments, plenty of doubts. But I just had to force myself to keep thinking "someday . . ."

Deb: And that "someday" is here. Oh, Kathy, I'm so

happy for you. Not only because you're getting a baby, but because you won't have to see any more agencies or doctors.

Kathy: *(jokingly)* It's a good thing, because there's certainly nothing left of this body that hasn't been poked, probed, or stared at by at least a hundred people. After a while I quit asking their name and just said, "Take me, I'm yours."

Deb: And then, finally, you get the call.

Kathy: I couldn't believe it; I was in shock. I stayed awake all night just to make sure it wasn't a dream. *(gets emotional)* And it's not; it's real. I just can't believe it.

Deb: How can that husband of yours work, knowing that in less than three hours he's going to be a father?

Kathy: I don't know, but I'm glad he's there and not here. We would have driven each other crazy.

Deb: Do you have a name for him?

Kathy: Uh huh. Jason. Jason Carter.

Deb: Oooh. I like that. Jason Carter. It sounds strong.

Kathy: I think so, too.

Greg: *(enters smiling, but not happy)* Hi, everybody.

Kathy: Oh, hi, Honey. I mean, "Daddy." Couldn't stay at work, huh?

Greg: No.

Deb: Congratulations, Greg. I can't tell you how happy I am for you!

Greg: Thanks, Deb.

Kathy: Greg, look what Deb bought for little Jason. *(showing him the outfit)* Isn't it cute? Our own little Chicago Bear.

Greg: Yeah. Um, listen, Deb, if you don't mind, I'd like to talk with Kathy about something.

Deb: Oh, sure. I need to get home, anyway.

Kathy: I think I've got a nervous father on my hands. What do you think?

Deb: I think you're right. *(hugs them)* Oh, I'm so happy for you two.

Kathy: Thanks, Deb. I'll see you tomorrow.

Deb: You better believe it. Wild horses couldn't keep me away. *(exits)*

Kathy: Bye.

Greg: Bye, Deb.

Kathy: Isn't she a good friend?

Greg: Yeah, she's pretty special. Uh, Honey, I want you to come sit down. I need to talk to you about something.

Kathy: *(lightly)* Oh, my. This sounds serious.

Greg: Kathy, it's about the baby.

Kathy: *(still lightly)* Greg, I already know what you're going to say.

Greg: I don't think you do.

Kathy: Look, I know ever since we got the call I've been thinking too much about the baby, but, Honey, that will change. I promise I'm not going to become one of those mothers whose whole life revolves around her kid. It's just that right now it's all I can think about. I'm just so excited to see our dream finally come true.

Greg: Kathy, our lawyer called me at work a little while ago. The girl decided to keep the baby.

Kathy: *(shocked)* What?

Greg: She changed her mind.

Kathy: But she can't do that. She signed the papers.

Greg: She has three days after the birth to change her mind.

Kathy: But she can't do that. She promised.

Greg: Kathy, she *can* do it and she did. Now, you knew it was a possibility.

Kathy: Where's Taylor's number? A lawyer should be able to do something.

Greg: Kathy, I asked him and there's nothing he can do.

Kathy: What do you mean, you asked? You couldn't have, or he'd be doing something.

Greg: There's nothing he can do. It's already been done. Now please . . . *(He goes to hug her, she pulls away.)*

Kathy: I don't believe you. It was all worked out. We had a baby. In just three hours he would be ours. He *is* ours.

Greg: *(trying to console her)* There will be other babies.

Kathy: Other babies? I don't want other babies. I want *this* one.

Greg: Well, we can't have him, Honey.

Kathy: *(pause)* I can't take this anymore. What does he want from us?

Greg: Who?

Kathy: God, that's who.

Greg: Honey, I don't think this is his fault.

Kathy: Well, who's fault is it, then? He's the one I've been praying to for nine years asking for a child. But does he give me one? No. My body remains sterile, and all the agencies keep saying, "We just don't have anything for you." And now this. Dangling a carrot in front of my nose only to yank it away. Well, I can't take it anymore.

Greg: *(crossing to her)* Honey.

Kathy: *(pulling away)* Leave me alone. *(Pause. Greg crosses to couch, starts to put baby outfit back in the box.)* What are you doing?

Greg: I'm putting this away. We've got to take it back.

Kathy: How can you think about taking it back now?

Greg: Kathy, what do you want me to think about?

Kathy: Our baby!

Greg: We don't have a baby.

Kathy: Shut up! Just shut up. I don't want to hear it. I'm tired of hearing it.

Greg: Honey, please, just calm down. *(grabbing on to her)*

Kathy: *(struggling to get free of him)* I don't want to calm down. I'm angry. I hate that girl. I hate you. I hate me. I hate God. I hate everybody. I hate this, I hate this, I hate this. *(Breaks down crying in Greg's arms.)*

Greg: *(long pause)* Come on. Let's sit down. *(They cross to couch, sit.)*

Kathy: *(broken)* Oh, Greg. Where have our prayers been going? Why isn't God listening? Is there some sin in our lives? Are we doing something wrong? How long do we have to keep praying?

Greg: *(simply, somewhat defeated as well)* As long as it takes.

Kathy: But I don't have any faith left. I'm empty. Oh, Greg, what are we going to do?

Greg: I don't know, Honey. *(slowly)* We'll just keep praying . . . keep trying. *(holds her close, tearful)* We'll just keep trying.

Lights fade slowly.

These Parts

One day a stranger appears in These Parts who tells an impaired family they can be whole. He offers them the gifts of sight, hearing, and the use of both arms. When the family consults the "experts," they discover such promises are impossible, and the stranger is killed. Even after he returns to life, he is rejected. Only the child remains and receives him.

SUGGESTED TOPICS: the Resurrection, basic Christianity, Easter

CHARACTERS:

Narrator	Doctor
Father	Scientist
Mother	Professor
Child	Stranger

PROPS: six arm slings, six eye patches, six ear patches (cotton and elastic "ear muffs" that fit over one ear)

These Parts

Judson Poling

Setting: An empty stage. The sketch begins with the seven characters standing upstage, backs to the audience. As the unseen narrator introduces the characters, they turn and cross toward the audience on their lines.

Narrator: Once upon a time there was a family who lived in a land called "These Parts." There was the dad . . .

Dad: Hi.

Narrator: The mother . . .

Mom: Hello.

Narrator: And the child . . .

Child: Hi.

Narrator: For as long as anyone could remember, everyone who lived in These Parts had a patch on one eye . . .

Dad: *(to wife)* Your patch looks lovely today, dear.

Narrator: A pad on one ear . . .

Mom: *(to husband)* Let me help straighten your pad, Honey.

Narrator: And one arm in a sling.

Child: Mommy, why do I have to wear this thing?

Narrator: Sometimes in These Parts, children asked very impolite questions!

Also living in the land were important advisors. There was the Scientist . . .

Scientist: Hello.

Narrator: The scholar . . .

Scholar: How do you do?

Narrator: And the doctor . . .

Doctor: Feeling well, I trust!

Narrator: *(as family and advisors cross toward each other, mingling and greeting)* Unfortunately, the people in These Parts were only part persons because of their patches, pads, and slings. But they'd been part people for so long, they hardly even noticed. That is, until one day, when a stranger came into town . . .

Stranger: *(turning, facing audience from upstage center)* Hello, everybody. I'm a stranger to These Parts!

Child: Mommy, what's a stranger?

Mom: Well, sweetheart, it's someone who . . . well, who's . . . strange.

Narrator: *(As the other characters move in for a closer look)* The stranger *was* different. He had no patch on his eye, no pad on his ear, and he could hug with both arms.

Stranger: Folks, I have great news for everyone living in These Parts. You don't have to be half blind, half deaf, and walk around with your arm in a sling. I can make you whole!

Narrator: The people in These Parts gasped at the startling news.

All: *(overdramatic in unison)* Gasp!

Dad: Now wait a minute—you mean to tell me you can make me see with two eyes?

Mom: And hear with two ears?

Child: And hug with two arms?

Stranger: Precisely. And I can do even more. You're not just part-people on the outside, but part-people on the inside, too. But I can change all that.

Mom: I don't know . . . change sounds pretty scary.

Dad: I've gotten along just fine with one eye; what do I need another one for?

Child: Mommy, why do I have to keep wearing this sling?

Stranger: *(to the child)* You don't sweetheart. Just follow me.

Mom: Now wait just a minute, Mister. Who do you think you are coming here and trying to poison our children with all your empty promises?

Stranger: But my promises are real. I come from a holy land where everyone is whole.

Narrator: And so they turned to the experts, those learned advisors, for guidance.

Dad: Ms. Scientist, tell us . . . can a person use two eyes, two ears, and both arms?

Scientist: Well, I've done calculations and consulted all known laws of physics, and I'm afraid it's impossible so . . . it can't happen.

Mom: Mr. Historian?

Scholar: I've studied ancient cultures and scoured the pages of recorded history, and I'm afraid it's never happened before so . . . it never happens.

Mom: What do you think, Doctor?

Doctor: I've examined many patients and kept accurate charts, and I'm afraid it's biologically unprecedented so . . . it doesn't happen.

Stranger: Do you prefer to be blind? Is it really that wonderful to be deaf?

Dad: Are we going to stand here and let this stranger insult us?

Scientist: Young man, you're not wanted here.

Scholar: You're upsetting the masses.

Doctor: Your words could destabilize life as we know it.

Dad: Let's get him out of here!!

Narrator: *(as the five characters grab the stranger, with the child standing off observing)* And so they set upon the stranger with the full force of their fury.

(Each grabs the stranger as he or she speaks.)

Scientist: You want us to have two eyes, huh?

Scholar: Well, see how you get along without any eyes.

Doctor: You think you can hear better than us?

Mom: We'll just scream in your ears till you can't hear at all!

Dad: You don't think I'm doing a good enough job loving my family? Well, just see how much you can do with your arms broken!

(The group hauls the stranger up center stage, and during the following narration they kill him in a stylized, slow-motion movement. The stranger ends up sitting on the floor, back to the audience, with the others in a circle around him.)

Narrator: In their rage, no one bothered to notice that every quality the stranger promised he also possessed. All they could think about was getting rid of his disquieting presence, and before they even knew what they were doing, they had killed the stranger.

Scholar: *(backing out of the circle somberly, trying to rationalize)* Well, he deserved it, you know?

Mom: *(same)* I couldn't really see what was happening.

Scientist: *(same)* Did you hear anything?

Dad: I have only one arm— surely it wasn't my blow that— *(He can't say "killed him.")*

Child: *(upset)* Mommy! *(Mom crosses to console her/ him.)*

Narrator: Almost as quickly as the tragedy happened, the family returned to life as usual in These Parts. No one wanted to talk about the stranger, or what they'd done to him. No one that is, except . . .

Stranger: *(crossing down center)* Hi everybody, I'm back!

Narrator: They couldn't believe their eye!

Dad: Who are you?

Stranger: You don't know?

Mom: But you look like . . .

Stranger: I am!

Doctor: But we . . .

Stranger: You did!

Scholar: But how can you be . . .

Stranger: Good question!

Scientist: But that's . . .

Stranger: You're right!

Scientist: But I've done calculations . . .

Scholar: I've studied civilizations . . .

Doctor: I've examined many patients . . .

Scientist: At laws I've looked—

Scholar: I've opened books—

Doctor: Their pulse I took—

Scientist: It can't happen!

Scholar: It never happens!

Doctor: It doesn't happen!

Stranger: It did happen! Look, it's not very scientific, or scholarly, or therapeutic to ignore evidence. Look, I'm here.

Mom: C'mon Dear, let's get out of here.

Dad: We shouldn't listen to wackos like this. *(They cross with the child to original positions.)*

Scientist: Dead men living . . . impossible! *(crosses to original position)*

Scholar: Unprecedented! *(same)*

Doctor: Unnatural! *(same)*

Child: *(after brief pause, turns from upstage position and slowly crosses to the stranger)* Mister, are you sure you're alive?

Stranger: *(tenderly)* What do you think?

Child: Well, yeah, you look okay, but I'm just a kid . . . what do I know?

Stranger: You know plenty.

Child: Uh, aren't you pretty mad at my mom and dad . . . I mean, after what they did to you?

Stranger: I know this is hard to believe, but my offer still stands for them. You too. *(pause)* Would you like my help?

Child: *(after thinking)* Yeah. Yeah, I would.

Stranger: What do you say we start with the sling?

Child: *(a bit cautious)* Okay. *(The stranger helps take off the sling.)*

Stranger: There. What do you think? *(Child sees his/her arm works fine, looks at stranger, then hugs him.)*

Child: You're right . . . it *does* feel better to hug with both arms!

Blackout

Other Willow Creek Resources Available

An Inside Look at the Willow Creek Seeker Service Video

An Inside Look at the Willow Creek Worship Service Video

One-on-One with Oliver North Video (an interview with Bill Hybels)

Sunday Morning Live, Volume 1

Sunday Morning Live Video, Volume 1

Sunday Morning Live Video, Volume 2

Walking With God Journal

Walking With God Series

   Building Your Church
   Discovering the Church
   "Follow Me!"
   Friendship With God
   Impacting Your World
   The Incomparable Jesus
   Leader's Guide 1
   Leader's Guide 2

Individual Drama Sketches Available

A listing and description of the over 200 Willow Creek drama sketches is now available from Willow Creek Resources™. These sketches provide a visually powerful way to introduce and reinforce a variety of biblical topics of interest to seekers and believers alike. Each is written to correspond with a message given by the pastor.

To obtain a free copy of this catalog, or for more information, call 1-800-876-SEEK (7335).